HOLY CITIES

VARANASI

Anita Ganeri

Evans Brothers Limited

Published by Evans Brothers Limited
2A Portman Mansions
Chiltern Street
London W1M 1LE

First published 1993

Printed in Hong Kong by Wing King Tong Co. Ltd.

ISBN 0 237 51270 X

ACKNOWLEDGEMENTS

Editorial: Catherine Chambers and Jean Coppendale
Design: Monica Chia
Production: Peter Thompson

Maps: Jillian Luff of Bitmap Graphics

The author and publishers would like to thank:
Saviour Pirotta for his help in devising the Holy Cities
series.

Dr Rupert Snell, Department of Indology and Modern
Languages and Literatures of South Asia at the School of
Oriental and African Studies for his help and advice with
the text.

Bipinchandra J. Mistry for all his help and advice and for the
use of his photographs.

For permission to reproduce copyright material the author
and publishers gratefully acknowledge the following:

Front cover: Main photograph – A scene on the
Dasaswamedh Ghat; inset left – Flower sellers; inset right –
Ganesha, the elephant god – Bipinchandra J. Mistry

Back cover: The sunken Shiv Temple – Bipinchandra J.
Mistry

Endpapers: Front – A ghat scene with Hindu temples
behind; Back – A Hindu boy receives a blessing from a
Brahmin priest at the shrine to Gang Mata – Bipinchandra J.
Mistry

Title page: Ganesha, the elephant god, with his 'vehicle', a
rat, by his side – Bipinchandra J. Mistry

Contents page: Shiva and Parvati with the bull, Nandi, in
the background – Ann and Bury Peerless

All the photographs in this book have been reproduced with
the permission of Bipinchandra J. Mistry, with the exception
of page 15 (bottom right) and page 32 (top), which have
been supplied by Ann and Bury Peerless.

Contents

The meanings of the words in **bold** can be found in the Key word boxes at the end of each chapter

The city between two rivers

The city of Varanasi lies on the west bank of the River Ganges in the north Indian state of Uttar Pradesh. It is the holiest city of the Hindus. About 800,000 people live in Varanasi but millions of pilgrims flock there every year to bathe in the sacred waters of the Ganges and to worship at the city's thousands of temples and shrines.

Varanasi is a busy, lively city full of noise and hustle and bustle. The city stretches from Raj **Ghat** in the north to Asi Ghat in the south. Behind the *ghats* lies a maze of narrow alleyways, called *galis*. These are lined with houses, temples and shrines. At stalls, people sell brass pots, copies of the holy books and flower garlands and many other things.

The name Varanasi is said to come from the names of two small rivers, the Varana and the Asi, which flow into the Ganges. The city lies between the two. According to legend, the rivers were put there by the gods to

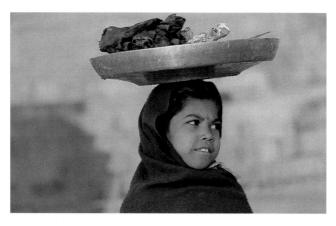

Waiting on the riverfront with coals for making a fire.

guard the holy city. Varanasi is also known as Benares or Banaras, which are simply versions of the name, Varanasi. Its oldest name is Kashi, which means 'City of Light' and describes its special sacred quality.

Key words

ghat a landing-step by the river or a place for cremating, or burning, the dead

Early morning bathers on the ghats in Varanasi.

India and the world

Varanasi and the other holy Hindu cities

N

PAKISTAN

Hardwar
R. Ganges
Delhi
NEPAL
Mathura
UTTAR
PRADESH
Ayodhya
R. Yamuna
R. Ganges
Varanasi
BHUTAN
BANGLADESH
BURMA

Dwarka
Ujjain
Calcutta

I N D I A

Bombay

- ● Hindu holy city
- ● Other city
- ---- State boundary
- —— Country boundary

Madras
Kanchipuram

| 0 | km | 500 |
| 0 | miles | 300 |

SRI
LANKA

Varanasi is one of seven Hindu holy cities, but it is the most sacred of them all.

Spires in a temple south of Asi Ghat on the outskirts of Varanasi.

— 7 —

City of Light – City of Shiva

Varanasi is one of the most ancient cities in the world. Although no one knows exactly when the city was founded, it was already a thriving, well-established settlement by the time the Buddha, the founder of the Buddhist religion, visited it in the early 6th century BC. At about the same time, the city had become the capital of the small kingdom of Kashi and was an important trading centre. Kashi was one of 16 kingdoms established in north India by the Aryans. These were a people from north-west Asia who had invaded India in about 1500 BC. They lived by farming and trading.

The kingdoms fought amongst themselves for control, and by the 5th century BC, they had been reduced to four. These came under the supreme rule of Kashi's neighbour, the kingdom of Magadha. The name 'Kashi' was now given to the city itself. Kashi grew and prospered. Between the 4th and 6th centuries AD, it became a respected centre of Hindu learning and culture, attracting students from all over India. It continued to flourish over the next few centuries, under a series of Hindu rulers.

The invasion of Varanasi

In AD 1194, disaster struck. The city was seized by Muslim invaders and hundreds of temples and shrines were destroyed. In their

The Great Mosque of the Mughal emperor, Aurangzeb.

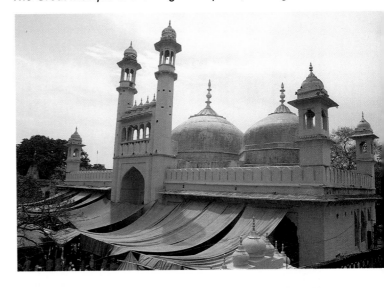

A statue of the Buddha in the Tibetan temple at Sarnath, the Buddhist holy city close to Varanasi.

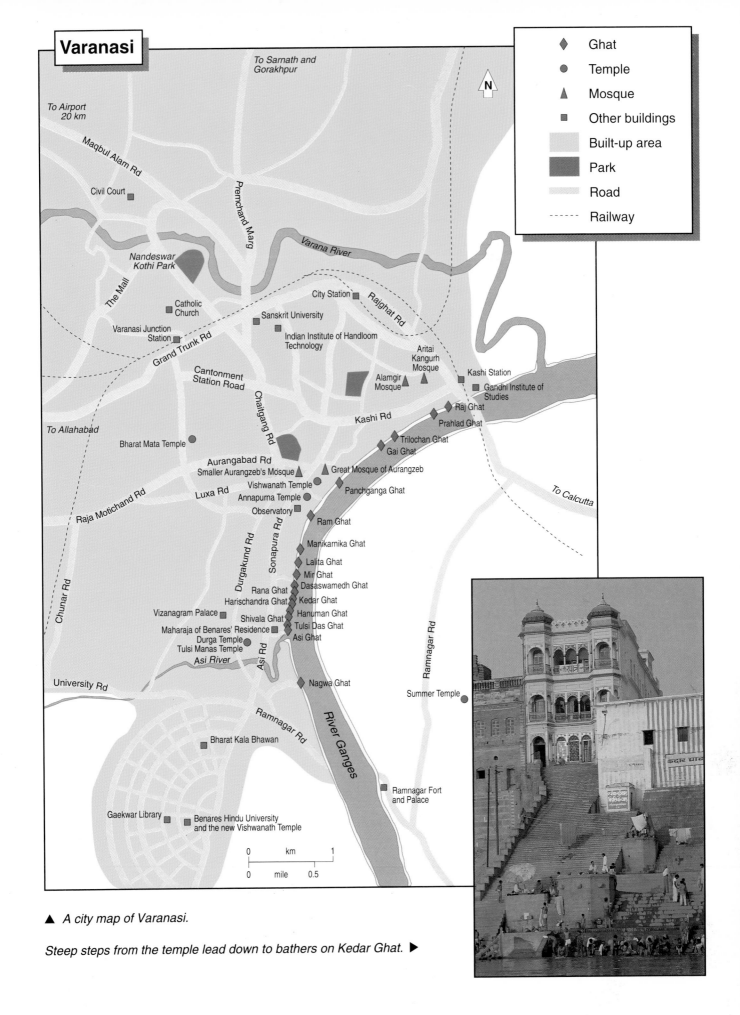

Varanasi

◆	Ghat
●	Temple
▲	Mosque
■	Other buildings
	Built-up area
	Park
	Road
- - -	Railway

N

To Sarnath and
Gorakhpur

To Airport
20 km

Maqbul Alam Rd

Civil Court

Premchand Marg

Varana River

Raighat Rd

Nandeswar
Kothi Park

The Mall

Catholic
Church

City Station

Varanasi Junction
Station

Sanskrit University

Grand Trunk Rd

Indian Institute of Handloom
Technology

Cantonment
Station Road

Aritai
Kangurh
Mosque

Kashi Station

Alamgir
Mosque

Gandhi Institute of
Studies

To Allahabad

Chaitgang Rd

Kashi Rd

Raj Ghat

Bharat Mata Temple

Prahlad Ghat

Aurangabad Rd

Trilochan Ghat

Smaller Aurangzeb's Mosque

Gai Ghat

Great Mosque of Aurangzeb

Luxa Rd

Vishwanath Temple

Panchganga Ghat

Annapurna Temple

Raja Motichand Rd

Observatory

Ram Ghat

Durgakund Rd

Sonapura Rd

Manikarnika Ghat

Lalita Ghat

Mir Ghat

Rana Ghat

Dasaswamedh Ghat

Harischandra Ghat

Kedar Ghat

Vizanagram Palace

Hanuman Ghat

Shivala Ghat

Tulsi Das Ghat

Maharaja of Benares' Residence

Asi Ghat

Chunar Rd

Durga Temple

Tulsi Manas Temple

Asi River

Asi Rd

Ramnagar Rd

University Rd

Summer Temple

Nagwa Ghat

River Ganges

To Calcutta

Ramnagar Rd

Bharat Kala Bhawan

Ramnagar Fort
and Palace

Gaekwar Library

Benares Hindu University
and the new Vishwanath Temple

0	km	1
0	mile	0.5

▲ A city map of Varanasi.

Steep steps from the temple lead down to bathers on Kedar Ghat. ▶

— 9 —

The Muslims built many mosques over Hindu temples.

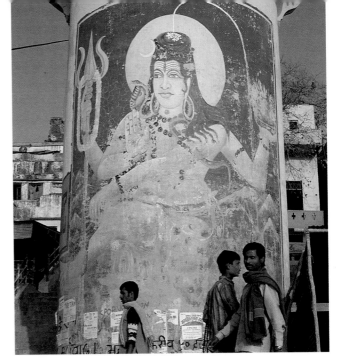
A painting of the great Hindu god, Shiva.

place, the Muslim rulers often built their own mosques (see page 25). But the great Mughal emperor, Akbar (1556-1605), encouraged and helped Hindus to rebuild their temples. His grandson, Aurangzeb, was not so lenient. During his reign (1658-1707), many temples were destroyed once again.

By the late 18th century, the Mughal empire had fallen apart and most of India came under British rule. Large areas of Varanasi, including temples and *ghats*, were rebuilt with money donated by the Marathas, the Hindu rulers of the region around Bombay. Very few of the temples you can see in Varanasi today are over 200 years old, although they may stand on the sites of much more ancient buildings. India became an independent country in 1947.

A view over the sacred River Ganges from Asi Ghat.

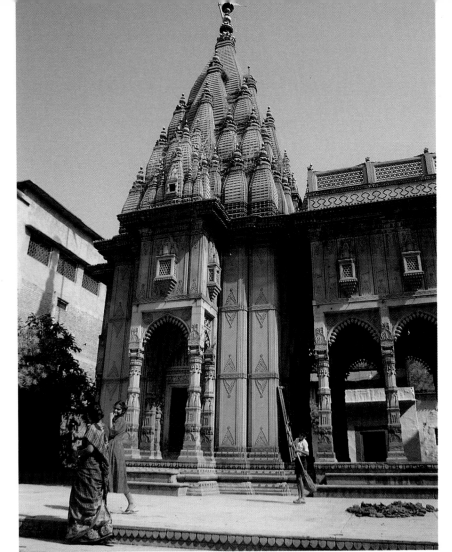

One of the many temples in Varanasi dedicated to the god Shiva.

The position of Varanasi on the River Ganges makes it even more important. The River Ganges is sacred to Hindus. They believe that bathing in its waters will wash away their sins. It is especially sacred and powerful at Varanasi. **Devout** Hindus try to visit Varanasi at least once in their lifetimes to bathe in the river. It is even more favourable to die in the city and be **cremated** on the banks of the river. By doing this, a person achieves *moksha*.

The most holy city

Varanasi is one of seven sacred Hindu cities in India. The other six are Ayodhya, Mathura, Hardwar, Ujjain, Kanchipuram and Dwarka. These are known in **Hindi** as *tirthas*, or 'crossing places' from this world to *moksha*, which is **salvation** (see pages 12 and 13). Varanasi is considered to be the holiest of the *tirthas*. It combines the goodness of all the other *tirthas* put together.

It is said to be the place chosen by Lord Shiva, one of the greatest of the Hindu gods, as his home on Earth. He also chose it to stand at the centre of the Earth. According to Hindu tradition, when Shiva left his home on Mount Kailasha in the Himalayas and married the goddess Parvati, he needed to find them somewhere to live, and he chose Varanasi. Varanasi is known as the city of Shiva – there are hundreds of temples dedicated to Shiva all over the city.

Key words

BC the years before the birth of Jesus Christ

AD the years after Christ was born

Hindi the main language spoken in Varanasi, and Uttar Pradesh as a whole

salvation being saved from sin, and therefore becoming free

devout very religious

cremated burnt to ashes

Think and do

Find the position of the seven *tirthas* on the map on page 7. Try to find out why each one of them is thought to be sacred.

Hindu beliefs

About 80 per cent of India's population, some 675 million people, are Hindus. There are also many Hindus living abroad, in countries such as Britain, Malaysia and the Gulf states. Hindus do not see their religion as separate from their daily lives. They see it much more as a way of life, affecting everything they do. In fact, the word Hinduism, meaning the Hindu religion, was invented by the British as late as the 19th century. Hindus simply call their way of life *dharma*, which means a sense of duty.

Hinduism is different from religions such as Islam or Christianity. It has no founder figure, such as Jesus Christ, and no single holy book, such as the Christian Bible. A person cannot become a Hindu, you have to be born one. But it is an extremely practical and **flexible** religion, even if it is a little complicated. Hindus may worship one god, several gods or none at all. They may worship at a grand temple or at a small **shrine** in their home.

How Hinduism began

Hinduism is one of the oldest living religions. It developed gradually, from the time of the

Brahmin children in early morning prayer on Asi Ghat.

Indus Valley civilization in north-west India in about 2500 BC. Archaeologists have found many female statues, probably of a mother goddess, among the ruins of the Indus cities. There are also statues which may represent an early form of Shiva. The Indus civilization came to an end in about 1500 BC, with the arrival of the Aryans. Their ideas mixed with those of the Indus people and marked the next stage of the Hindu religion. The Aryans' religious hymns, collected together as the *Rig Veda*, are still among the holiest books of Hinduism (see page 39).

Puppets in the Tulsi Manas Temple act out scenes from one of the Hindu sacred texts, the Ramayana *(see page 40).*

श्री सीता स्वयंबर

The aims of Hinduism

Hindus believe in reincarnation. This means that you are reborn after you die. Reincarnation can happen many times, in a cycle of death and rebirth called *samsara*. The ultimate goal of a Hindu is to achieve *moksha*, or freedom from *samsara*. You can be reborn in many different forms, not necessarily in the same form as your previous life. If you have led a good life, you move closer to *moksha*. If you have acted badly in your

There are hundreds of small roadside shrines all over Varanasi.

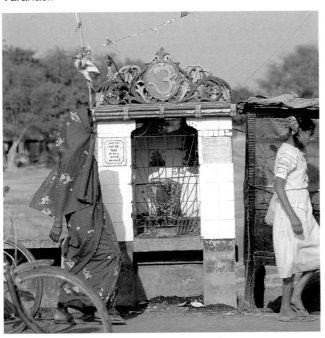

A stall selling prayer beads and incense.

previous life, you are reborn further away from *moksha*. Your actions and deeds, together with their results, are known as *karma*.

The caste system

From the time of the Aryans, Hindu society has traditionally been divided up into four classes, called castes. These were originally based on what type of work people did. The four castes are Brahmins (priests and teachers), Kshatriyas (soldiers and nobles), Vaishyas (traders and craftsmen) and Shudras (labourers and servants). A fifth group, the untouchables, were considered too lowly to be part of the caste system. They did the dirtiest, most menial tasks. Hindus are born into a particular caste and cannot change from one to another. But they can be reborn into a higher or lower caste, depending on their *karma*.

Key words

flexible easily changed; adaptable

shrine a holy place of worship, often with a sacred picture, ashes or other holy objects

Gods and goddesses

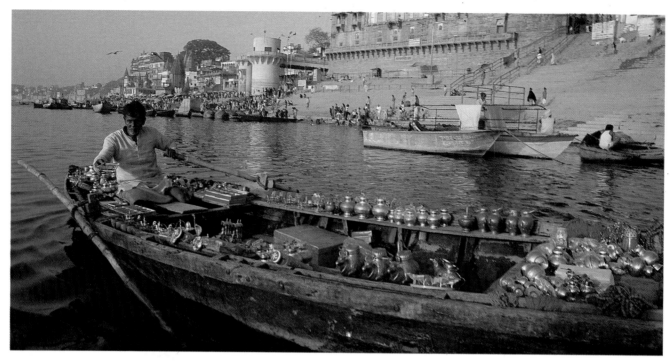

Hindus believe in a supreme being, called Brahman, who is found everywhere and in everything. Various **aspects** of Brahman are represented by the gods and goddesses. The three main gods are Brahma, Vishnu and Shiva. But there are also millions of others.

Gods and goddesses are shown in many ways, as pictures and as statues. Hindus do not worship the statue itself, but the aspect of the god or goddess it represents. The gods are shown with symbols which identify their special qualities. They also have a special animal, called a vehicle, associated with them.

A floating shop selling brass pots for pilgrims to carry Ganges water in and other items needed for worship.

There are pictures and **images** of the gods and goddesses everywhere in Varanasi. They are not just in the temples, but in the shops, hotels and even in taxis and **rickshaws**.

Brahma, the creator

Brahma has four faces for looking at all four corners of the Earth. He rides on a goose and is shown as a priestly figure, holding a rosary and a flask of holy water. His wife is the goddess of learning and arts, Saraswati. She rides on a white swan and carries a stringed musical instrument, called a *veena*.

Vishnu, the preserver

Vishnu is shown sitting on the coils of a giant serpent. In his four arms, he holds a conch shell, a discus, a sword and a trumpet as symbols of his great power and holiness. His vehicle is the half-man, half-eagle, Garuda. His wife is the goddess of wealth, Lakshmi.

The goddess Durga riding on her 'vehicle', the tiger.

You can buy statues of the gods from many wayside stalls.

The god Krishna, one of the forms taken by Vishnu on his visits to Earth.

From time to time, Vishnu visits the Earth to save it from evil. He has appeared nine times so far. On his seventh visit, he came as the hero, Rama (see page 41). On his eighth visit, he appeared as the god, Krishna. Both Rama and Krishna are worshipped throughout India.

Shiva, the destroyer

Shiva rides on a bull, called Nandi. He carries a trident – a symbol of destruction. He has a third eye in the middle of his forehead which represents knowledge. The River Ganges flows through his hair (see page 28). His wife, the goddess Parvati, is usually beautiful and good. But she also has a terrible side to her, as the goddess of battle, Durga. As Durga, she is shown with ten arms, each holding a weapon. She rides on a tiger.

Ganesha, the elephant god

The elephant-headed god, Ganesha, is the son of Shiva and Parvati, and is a very popular god of success and wisdom. He rides on a rat. Ganesha is also seen as a protector or guardian. You can see his image guarding many of the doorways of temples and homes in Varanasi. There are also 56 images of Ganesha in and around the city, to guard and protect it from evil. According to legend, Ganesha got his elephant head after an argument with Shiva. Ganesha was guarding the door while Parvati bathed, and refused to let anyone, even Shiva, inside. Shiva was furious and cut off Ganesha's head. He later **repented** and gave Ganesha the head of the first animal he saw – an elephant.

The elephant-headed god, Ganesha.

Key words

aspects forms or attitudes

images likenesses in the form of paintings or statues

rickshaws two-wheeled carriages pulled by a runner or a cyclist

repented showed sorrow for sins

Think and do

The vehicle for the goddess Durga, is a tiger. Why do you think this is so? Draw a picture of Durga in battle.

The Ganges and the ghats

If you take a boat trip along the river at Varanasi, you will not be able to miss the city's most famous and most visited feature. The river front has been carved into a series of long, often crumbling, steps, called *ghats*, which lead down into the sacred River Ganges. Pilgrims and residents of the city flock here every day to bathe and pray.

The holy Ganges

The Ganges is India's second longest river, rising in the Himalayas in the far north and flowing for about 2,500 kilometres until it reaches the Bay of Bengal, and the sea. For Hindus, the water of the Ganges is sacred right along its course. It washes away people's sins, allowing them to reach *moksha*.

The Ganges is heavily polluted with animal and human waste and the Indian government has set up an action plan to clean up the river. Despite pollution, pilgrims have no hesitation about bathing in the Ganges, such is its power. You may see them scooping up handfuls of water and then pouring it back into the river as an offering to the gods. They

This sadhu *is a follower of Shiva.*

also carry water home in special brass pots. The Ganges is worshipped as the goddess, Ganga, as well. On page 28, you can read about how Ganga came to Earth.

The ghats

The *ghats* stretch for about 7 kilometres along the river front at Varanasi, from Asi Ghat in the south to Raj Ghat in the north. There are

Stone linga, *the symbols of Shiva.*

Children enjoying the holy waters of the River Ganges.

about 100 sets of these long, stone steps. Some have crumbled or subsided into the river. When the monsoon rains come in July, the river is three times its normal width and rises some 15 metres up the riverbank. Many of the *ghats* and their temples are submerged until the water goes down in September. Then they have to be dug out of the piles of mud and silt which the river has deposited.

Many of the *ghats* are crowded with bathers, priests, *sadhus* (holy men), beggars, people doing **yoga** exercises or **meditating**, and even sacred cows (see page 34). There are temples and shrines at every step, including hundreds of *linga*, the symbols of Shiva (see page 22). There is plenty of noise, too – prayers are chanted, hymns are sung, and temple bells are rung.

Dawn on the ghats

The best time to visit the *ghats* is at dawn, the most favourable time for people to bathe in the river. This is the time when they greet the Sun as it rises. In legend, Shiva sent Surya, the Sun god, to Varanasi to be his ambassador there. Brahmin priests recite a morning prayer, called the Gayatri Mantra:

A Brahmin reciting the Gayatri Mantra, sitting in the yoga position called the lotus.

Sun worshippers on Asi Ghat.

'We meditate on the great glory of the divine Sun. May it inspire us.'

The priests sit under large umbrellas on the *ghat* steps. They look after the bathers' needs, performing rituals for them, looking after their clothes and preparing their horoscopes. In return, they are given a token offering of grain or money. In the past, the 'token' sometimes took the form of the gift of a cow.

There are also *sadhus*, who bathe and pray along the *ghats*. They have given up their homes, worldly goods and possessions to wander in search of spiritual salvation, relying on charity to live. Some are closely linked with a particular god. Followers of Vishnu wear three vertical lines of ash on their foreheads. Followers of Shiva wear three horizontal lines. The ash marks are called *tilakas* and are signs of devotion or blessing. These holy men may also carry tridents.

Sadhus use yoga exercises to help them concentrate their minds and control their bodies so that their souls can become one with

Pilgrims and priests on Dasaswamedh Ghat.

Brahman and achieve *moksha*. There are many types of yoga. One of the best known is *Hatha yoga*, which consists of physical exercises and special breathing to relax the body and clear the mind. The exercises, or postures, are called *asanas*. One of the most important is the *padma asana*, or lotus posture. A lotus is a large, white flower with open petals sacred to Hindus and Buddhists.

Along the ghats

Many of the stone *ghats* in Varanasi were built in the 18th century by the Marathas (see page 10). Others were built by wealthy princes and aristocrats, who still own them. These are some of the main ghats and the ways they are used:

Asi Ghat The Asi Ghat is one of the oldest and most important bathing *ghats* for

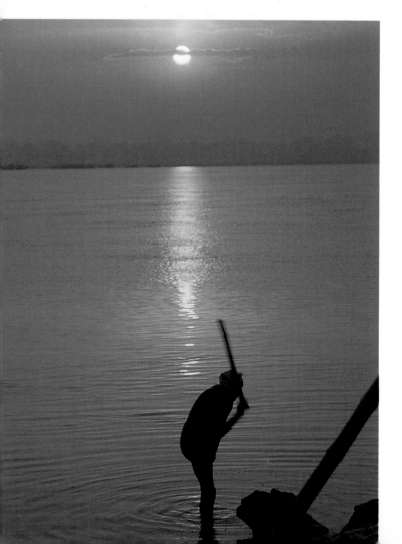

This dhobiwallah *(laundry man) is beating wet clothes in the river to get them clean. He will then lay them out on the steps of the* ghat *to dry.*

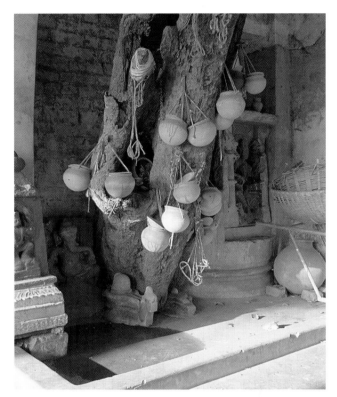

pilgrims. Unlike many of the other *ghats*, it has no steps. Instead, a slippery bank leads down the river.

Dhobi Ghat This is where the city's laundry is done. The *dhobiwallahs* (laundry men) soak

These clay pots contain the ashes of Hindus who have been cremated. They are ready for the priest to scatter on the River Ganges.

the clothes in the river, then slap them down on great wash slabs to get them clean. Then they spread them out in the Sun to dry.

Pilgrims on Dasaswamedh Ghat buying religious souvenirs.

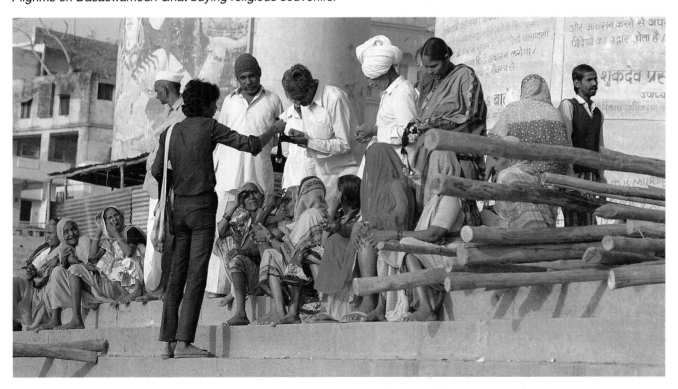

Man Mandir Ghat This *ghat* was built in 1600 by Maharaja Man Singh of Amber in Rajasthan. His royal palace still stands on the *ghat*. In 1710, the palace was converted into an observatory by Maharaja Jai Singh of Jaipur. He was famous for being a great warrior and a great astronomer.

Dasaswamedh Ghat This is the most popular, and the most crowded, of all the *ghats* in Varanasi. Its name means ten (*das*), horse (*aswa*), sacrifice (*medh*). You can read more about this on page 29. It is considered one of the holiest *ghats* to bathe in. A main road leads from the city down to Dasaswamedh Ghat. The road is lined with beggars, asking pilgrims for food and money. On the *ghat* itself, there is a temple to the goddess of smallpox, Shitala. Smallpox was a very dangerous disease.

Panchaganga Ghat Panchaganga Ghat is said to be the place where the five (*panch*) holy rivers meet – the Ganges, Saraswati, Yamuna, Kirana and Dhutpapa. A magnificent Hindu temple which once stood on the *ghat* was destroyed by Emperor

These piles of wood on Manikarnika Ghat will be used for building funeral pyres.

Aurangzeb, who built a mosque on top of it. The *ghat* has many small shrines which open out on to the river. Some are used for meditation. Others contain Shiva *linga* or sometimes images of gods and goddesses.

The burning ghats

Two of the *ghats* along the river are known as the 'burning *ghats*'. They are Harishchandra Ghat and Manikarnika Ghat. This is where people are cremated and their ashes scattered on the Ganges. People who die in Varanasi are thought to be extremely fortunate and blessed. They are assured of *moksha*. Old and sick people often come to Varanasi especially to end their days in the city. There are also people who never leave Varanasi for fear that they might die outside the holy city. Other pilgrims bring the ashes of their dead relatives to scatter on the river.

A body is brought down from the city on a bamboo stretcher, covered in a red or white cloth. The dead person's family chants and prays as it follows the procession down to the *ghat*. Then the body is dipped into the Ganges and put on the funeral pyre. Burning the body is the way of offering it to Agni, the god of fire. The funeral pyre is made of logs of sweet-smelling sandalwood or neem wood. It is lit by the eldest son, or a close relative, from an eternal flame which is always kept burning on the *ghat*. The ashes are later raked up and scattered on the river. After the cremation, there are 12 days of **rites** and **rituals** to ensure that the dead person's soul has a safe journey.

Harischandra Ghat is named after a king of ancient times. Despite his high **status**, he worked at the cremation grounds to prove his devotion to the god, Brahma (see page 28).

A place of pilgrimage

People travel from all over India, by coach, train and even on foot, to make a pilgrimage to Varanasi. They visit the temples, bathe in the river and may follow two special pilgrimage routes through the city and along the riverfront. Priests assist the pilgrims at every stage of their journey.

Panchakroshi The Panchakroshi pilgrimage follows a path around the outskirts of Varanasi. It starts at Manikarnika Ghat, follows the river to Asi Ghat, then runs in a large semi-circle to Adi Keshava Ghat. Pilgrims take about five to six days to complete the 56 kilometre journey. They visit 108 holy shrines on the way.

Panchaganga Ghat – one of the five stops on the Panchatirthi pilgrimage.

Panchatirthi This one-day pilgrimage leads along the *ghats* and the riverfront. Pilgrims have to stop and bathe at five (*panch*) holy crossing places (*tirth*). They are, in their set order, Asi Ghat, Dasaswamedh Ghat, the point where the Varana River flows into the Ganges, Panchaganga Ghat and finally, Manikarnika Ghat. Then the pilgrims turn into the city to worship in the most important temples.

Key words

yoga exercise and deep thought, which lead to peace and calmness

meditating thinking deeply

rites religious ceremonies, especially spoken or read from holy books

rituals performances of special rites

status position in society

Think and do

Describe the ways in which the people of Varanasi use the *ghats* and the waters of the Ganges. Can you think of any other uses that have not been mentioned in this chapter?

The temples of Varanasi

There are at least 1,500 temples in Varanasi and thousands more small shrines. There are temples along the riverfront, at the top of the *ghats*, and in and around the city itself. Most Hindu temples are dedicated to one particular god or goddess. Since this is the city of Shiva, most temples and shrines in Varanasi are dedicated to Lord Shiva. But for pilgrims, a trip to Varanasi provides the opportunity to visit other temples as well, each with its own gods and characteristics. Many of Varanasi's most ancient temples were destroyed by the Muslims (see page 9). Some of the present temples have been built very recently.

Shiva linga

Wherever you go in Varanasi, you will see simple columns of stone, called *linga*. These represent Shiva and are symbols of his power and presence. In temples dedicated to Shiva, *linga* are the focus of people's worship, rather than an image of Shiva himself. In the stalls

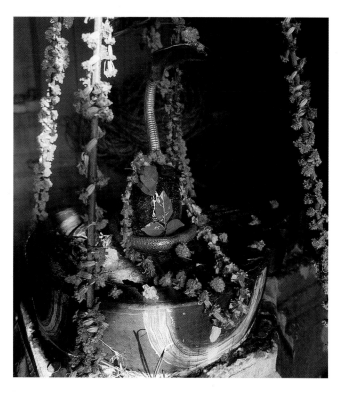

A *Shiva* lingam, *covered in offerings.*

around the temples in Varanasi, pilgrims can buy small *linga* to take home with them or to wear around their necks.

A street shrine to the monkey god, Hanuman.

A Shiva temple that has partly sunk into the riverbed.

The images of Rama and Sita inside a Shiva temple.

The Golden Temple

The Golden Temple gets its name from its gold covered spire. It is dedicated to Vishwanath, the name given to Shiva in his role as Lord of the Universe. This is the most sacred of all Varanasi's temples. It was built in 1776 by the Rani (Queen) of Indore and its golden spire was added in 1835. It stands near the site of the previous Vishwanath Temple, which was destroyed by Emperor Aurangzeb in 1669 (see page 9). In its place, he constructed the Jnana Vapi mosque. Traces of the Vishwanath Temple can be seen near the mosque. Next to the Golden Temple, is the Jnana Vapi (the Well of Knowledge). According to legend, this is where the Shiva *lingam* from the Vishwanath Temple was hidden for protection. Shiva is said to have dug the well himself with his trident.

The Bharat Mata Temple

The Bharat Mata Temple is dedicated to Mother (*Mata*) Bharat (*India*). Instead of an image of a god or goddess, it contains a huge marble map of India with all the sacred places marked on it. The temple was opened by the peace-loving Indian leader, Mahatma Gandhi.

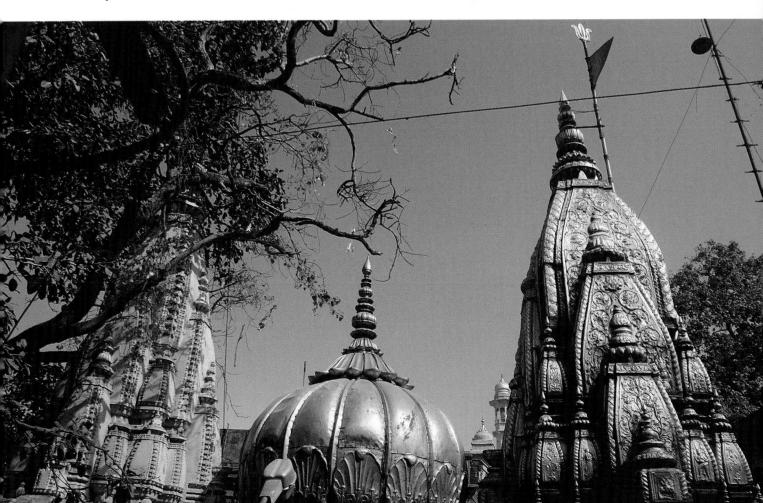

The gleaming spires of the Golden Temple, which is dedicated to Shiva as Vishwanath, Lord of the Universe.

The Annapurna Temple

The goddess Annapurna is the wife of Shiva in his role as Vishwanath (Lord of the Universe) and so is an extremely important figure in Varanasi. She is seen as a kind and gracious goddess who feeds and cares for her followers. Annapurna Temple stands quite close to the Golden Temple. It was built in the 18th century, but the image of the goddess inside is less than 20 years old. Another shrine in the temple contains a solid gold

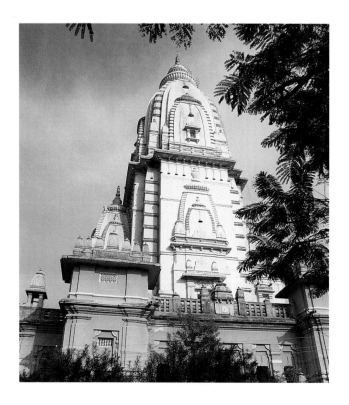

Worshippers at the Durga Temple or Monkey Temple. It is stained red with ochre clay.

image of the goddess. This shrine is only open for three days a year, at the time of the great festival of Annapurna (see page 32).

The Durga Temple

Durga Temple was built in the 18th century by a Bengali princess. It is often called the Monkey Temple because of the hundreds of monkeys which live in it. The temple is dedicated to Durga, the goddess of battle (see page 15). Two paintings of the goddess guard the entrance to the temple sanctuary, the most sacred part of the temple which contains the image of the goddess. The image is a silver mask, covered in a red cloth.

The New Vishwanath Temple

This modern temple was built near the Benares (Varanasi) Hindu University by the wealthy Birla family, in the middle part of this century. It is said to be a copy of the temple which Aurangzeb destroyed. Verses from the Hindu holy texts are inscribed on the walls of the temple.

The New Vishwanath Temple, built in the grounds of the Benares Hindu University. It is less than 100 years old.

The mosques of Varanasi

Although Varanasi is the holy city of the Hindus, a large number of Muslims live in it. Two of Aurangzeb's 17th century mosques are also still standing – the Jnana Vapi mosque, or the Great Mosque of Aurangzeb, and the mosque of Alamgir. Both were built on the site of Hindu temples. The remains of these temples can still be seen. The Jnana Vapi mosque has **minarets** which tower some 70 metres above the River Ganges.

The Tulsi Manas Temple

Tulsi Manas Temple is a modern temple, built in 1964 in honour of the great poet, Tulsi Das who lived in Varanasi in the late 16th and early 17th centuries. His epic poem, *Ram Charit Manas*, is written in black marble on the white marble walls of the temple. *Ram Charit Manas* tells the story of the god, Rama, and his wife, Sita. It is based on a version of the ancient sacred book, the *Ramayana*. You can find out more about this and about Tulsi Das, on page 41.

The Alamgir Mosque, built by Emperor Aurangzeb.

Key words

minarets   towers from which the call to prayer is made

The white marble Tulsi Manas Temple. It was built in 1964 on the site where the famous poet, Tulsi Das, lived.

A visit to the temple

A Hindu temple is usually separated from the outside world by a wall. You enter through a gateway in the wall. The main shrine is in the temple courtyard. The shrine contains the image of the god or goddess that is special to the temple. This is the holiest part of the temple. There may also be other, smaller shrines around it. The temple sometimes has a tank or well where worshippers can bathe before they worship.

In the temple, people take off their shoes, and women cover their heads as signs of respect.

Hindu temples are busy, bustling, lively and very noisy places. The smell of **incense** is everywhere. People sing hymns and chant the names of the gods, or passages from the holy books. Storytellers attract crowds of listeners. The temple is seen as the **deity's** home on Earth. It is sacred but it is full of life as well.

When a Hindu visits a temple, it is not simply to pray but to have the *darshana*, or 'sight' of the god or goddess. The worshippers bring offerings of Ganges water, fruit, sweets and flower garlands for the deity. All of these things can be bought from the stalls lining the streets leading to the temple. The priest places the offerings in contact with the image of the deity, in order

A bowl of red paste, used for applying the tilaka *to a worshipper's forehead.*

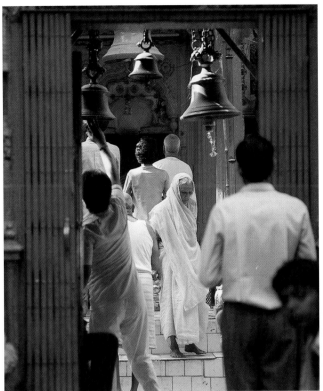

may also walk around the shrine as a mark of **reverence**. This is called circumambulation. People walk in a clockwise direction so that they always keep their favourable right hand facing the deity. The left hand is considered unclean. This is why Hindus only eat with their right hands.

There is no obligation for Hindus to go to the temple and there are different ways of worshipping in the different temples. Many perform daily *puja*, or worship, at home and only visit the temple occasionally. But the whole family is welcome in the temple, and children learn about the gods and goddesses by taking part in the *puja* and by listening to their parents and grandparents.

to bless them. Then he gives some back to the worshippers to **bestow** the god's grace on them. These offerings are known as *prasada*.

The priest also marks the worshippers' foreheads with a *tilaka* of blessing (see page 18). A tray of small lamps, called *arati*, may be circled in front of the god. Worshippers

Offerings needed for puja. *The trays at the back contain sweets.*

Key words

incense	strong smelling spices or wood
deity	god or goddess
bestow	offer as a gift
reverence	deep respect

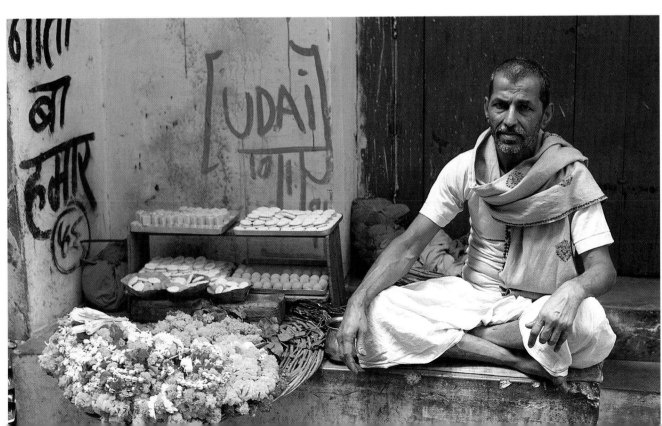

Legends and traditions

There are many legends about the gods and goddesses, and about places in Varanasi. These are just a few of them.

How the Ganges fell to Earth

There are several legends explaining how the Ganges, the 'river of heaven', came to Earth. An ancient king, called Bhagiratha, asked Brahma to let the Ganges fall from the sky to bring his 60,000 **ancestors** back to life. They had been turned to ashes by Vishnu thousands of years before (see page 15). But the king realized that the Earth would shatter under the force of the falling water. So Shiva agreed to catch the river in his hair to break its fall. Then Bhagiratha led the Ganges from the Himalayas where it fell across the plains, bringing the king's ancestors back to life.

The lost earring

Above the steps of the Manikarnika Ghat, there is a sacred tank of water called the Manikarnika Well. According to legend, Vishnu dug the well with his discus and filled it with his sweat. Then he sat down by the well and meditated for 500,000 years. One day, he was visited by Shiva and Parvati (see page 11). Shiva was so pleased by Vishnu's devotion that he shook with delight and his

jewelled earring fell into the well. This gave the *ghat* its name. The word *manikarnika* means 'jewel of the earring'.

Vishnu's footprints

Between the well and the steps of Manikarnika Ghat, there is a large slab of stone. This is said to bear the footprints of Vishnu and to mark the spot where he meditated for so many years. Pilgrims always stop to worship here, sprinkling the footprints with sacred Ganges water and laying down offerings of flower garlands. A few very important people, such as the **Maharajas** of Varanasi, are allowed to be cremated here.

A small boy praying in front of Shiva, who has earrings in both ears.

The bull, Nandi, Shiva's special animal. He sits close to the Manikarnika Well, which he guards. He is visited by many pilgrims.

Varanasi. Shiva was sure that Divodasha would get the ceremony wrong, allowing Shiva to return. But the king made no mistakes at all. The sacrifice went smoothly and so Shiva was kept out of Varanasi.

Dasaswamedh Ghat, where the ten horse sacrifice is said to have taken place.

The ten horse sacrifice

The name of the Dasaswamedh Ghat comes from the Hindi words for 'ten horse sacrifice' (see page 20). This refers to a very ancient tradition which was used to strengthen the power and position of a ruling king. Ten horses were allowed to wander freely. Wherever they wandered, this land could be claimed by the king as his own.

Varanasi was once ruled by a king called Divodasha. He had agreed to rule as long as the gods left the city and allowed him to get on with his task. But Shiva was determined to return. He sent Brahma to Varanasi to perform a ceremony called the ten horse sacrifice. Divodasha was told that he had to provide everything needed, and assist Brahma with the ceremony. If Divodasha made a mistake, then Shiva could return to

Key words

ancestors grandparents, great grandparents and so on

Maharajas great Indian princes

Think and do

If you were a pilgrim how many places would you visit at Manikarnika Ghat? Why are these places important?

Festivals and celebrations

▲ Parents have no control over their children during Holi!

◄ These coloured powders are mixed with water and splashed over people during Holi.

There are hundreds of Hindu festivals throughout the year, which for Hindus begins in March or April. Some are celebrated all over India; others are special to certain places, such as Varanasi. Of course, no one is expected to celebrate every festival – they would never have time for anything else! Pilgrims to Varanasi can buy a special festival guide to help them plan their stay. There are also family celebrations during the year.

A festival of spring

In March or April, the lively festival of Holi marks the beginning of spring. On the night before Holi, people build bonfires and burn models of the witch, Holika. In legend, she tried to kill her nephew, Prahlada, because he was a follower of Vishnu. But Holika was killed instead. The next morning, people celebrate by splashing each other with coloured water and powders. It is wise to wear your oldest clothes! In the afternoon, people bathe in the Ganges. Then, in the evening, they visit relatives and friends with gifts of sweets.

Getting drenched with coloured water is an important part of the Holi festivities!

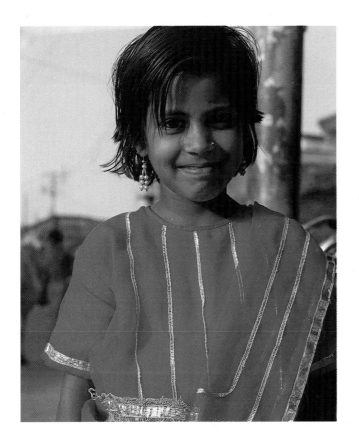

All dressed up, ready to visit friends and family on Holi evening.

A festival of plays

The festival of Dussehra lasts for ten days in September. It is celebrated all over India, but in several different ways. In Varanasi, this is the time of the Ram Lila, a series of plays telling the story of Rama's life (see page 41). The plays are performed in many places including Ramnagar Fort, the home of the Maharaja of Varanasi.

At the end of the play, Rama kills the demon king, Ravana. The actor playing Rama shoots a flaming arrow into a huge paper and bamboo model of Ravana. The model is full of exploding firecrackers. The Maharaja arrives at the final night's performance on an elephant's back (see photograph on page 32).

On the day after Rama's victory, the Bharat Milap festival takes place in Varanasi. This marks the return of Rama to his home in Ayodhya and his reunion with his brother, Bharata, whom he has not seen for 14 years.

The lights of Diwali

Diwali is celebrated at the end of October or the beginning of November. It lasts for five days. Diwali means the 'festival of lights' because there are lights and fireworks everywhere you go. The lights are intended to guide Rama home after his long exile (see page 41). Diwali is also dedicated to the goddess of fortune, Lakshmi. People leave their doors open so that Lakshmi can come inside. They keep a lamp shining to help her find her way. This is also the time when business people close their old account books and start new ones. In Varanasi, people float strings of oil lamps in little clay pots down the Ganges.

A mountain of food

The day after Diwali is known as Annakuta, which means 'mountain of food'. This day is celebrated all over India, in honour of Krishna. But in Varanasi, it is also the time of a great festival to the goddess Annapurna (see page 24). At the Annapurna Temple, the shrine containing the golden image of the goddess is opened for *darshana*, and the temple is filled with food. This is offered to the goddess, then given out to people as *prasada* (see page 27).

The arrival of the Maharaja on his elephant during the Ram Lila festival.

The night of Mahashivaratri

The night of the full moon in the month of Phalguna is called Mahashivaratri, the Great Night of Shiva. This is one of the most important nights of the year in Varanasi, the city of Shiva. People sing hymns in praise of Shiva and visit the most important temples and *linga* for *darshana* (see pages 22 and 26). On the day of Mahashivaratri, the whole family **fasts** – except for eating some sweets or fruit.

The goddess of wealth and fortune, Lakshmi, is worshipped during Diwali.

The ghats are crowded with worshippers on the night of Mahashivaratri.

Family celebrations

Hindus also have many ceremonies and celebrations to mark special events in their lives. When a baby is born, there is a ceremony to mark its arrival into the world. Ten days later, there is another ceremony at which the baby is given its name and its horoscope is made by a priest.

On Mahashivaratri, priests perform puja *to Shiva. The* puja *is taking place on Dasaswamedh Ghat.*

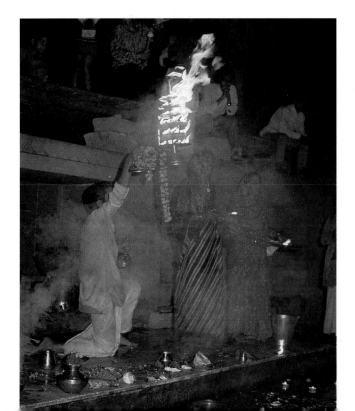

When boys belonging to the top three castes (Brahmin, Kshatriya and Vaishya) reach between the ages of nine and eleven, there is a very special ceremony. This is when a boy receives his 'sacred thread' from the priest. The thread is looped over the boy's left shoulder and under his right arm. This marks the next stage in his life, when he begins to learn more about his religion.

A Hindu wedding is extremely important to a family. Most weddings are 'arranged', which means that the bride and groom are chosen for each other by their families. A wedding lasts several days. Each day has its own rituals and ceremonies. In Varanasi, they include the bride and groom bathing in the River Ganges.

Key words

fasts stops eating food, or certain foods, for a particular time

Daily life in Varanasi

▲ *The bustling Dasaswamedh Road, leading down to the ghats.*

The people of Varanasi are proud of living in their city. It is a bright, intriguing place which not only attracts pilgrims from all over India but is visited by thousands of tourists every year. It takes a little while to get used to the noise and crowds, but there are plenty of interesting things to see.

The streets of the city are packed with people, vehicles, rickshaws and cows. Hindus

▼ *Sacred cows wander freely around Varanasi.*

Flowers sellers with garlands of marigolds, roses and jasmine.

Weaving one of Varanasi's famous silk saris.

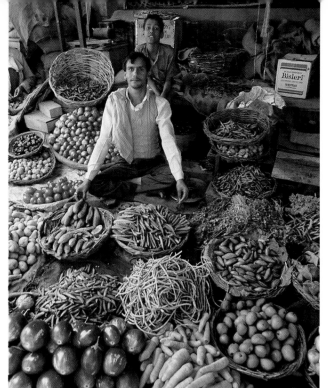

A street stall selling fresh vegetables.

consider cows to be sacred animals. They never harm or kill them and they never eat beef. All over India, it is quite normal to see cows sitting down in the middle of the street, blocking the traffic. Varanasi is no exception! In the heart of the city lies a maze of narrow alleyways. It would be easy to get lost in them. They are so narrow that you have to press up against a wall if a funeral procession passes by on its way to the burning ghats.

The main streets and the alleyways are lined with stalls and shops. Some sell the items needed for *puja* – garlands of flowers such as marigolds and jasmine, prayer beads, oil lamps, incense, prayer books and religious trinkets. There are also stalls selling fresh fruit and vegetables.

Silk and saris

Since ancient times, Varanasi has been famous for its crafts. Two of the main craft industries today are sari-making and carpet-making. Varanasi is the centre of carpet-making in India, and most of the carpets are sold abroad. Hindu women traditionally get married in silk saris. If they can afford it, they wear silk saris made from Varanasi silk. These are famous for the gold or silver

▲ *Varanasi is an important centre of classical Indian music.*

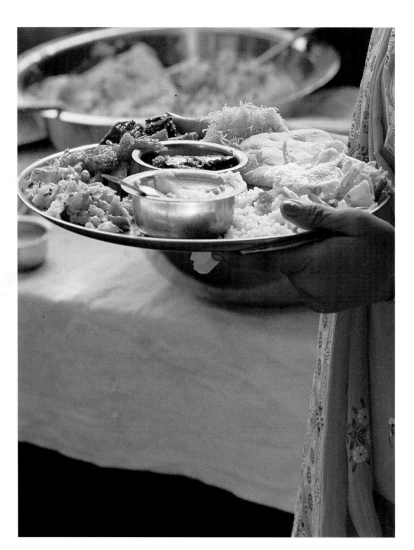

embroidery on them. This is called *zari* work. It is mostly produced by Muslim craftsmen, using very fine threads of metal. Buyers come to Varanasi from all over India to stock up with saris for their own shops.

Eating out in Varanasi

Some of the stalls lining the streets of Varanasi sell sizzling snacks, *pan* (see page 37), sweets and drinks. Most Hindus are vegetarians, especially in Varanasi and other holy places. A typical meal might consist of *dahl* (made of lentils), several spicy vegetable dishes and rice or round, flat bread, called *chapatti*. People eat with their right hand, often sitting on the floor.

Indian sweets are very popular. They are usually made of milk or rice, mixed with nuts. People give sweets as presents on special occasions, such as weddings and festivals.

A typical meal consists of small dishes which contain a variety of sweet and savoury food.

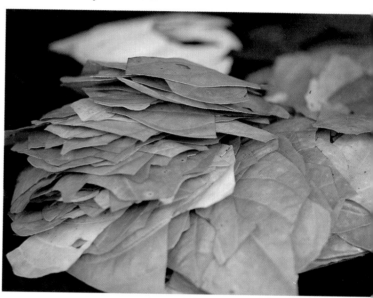

Pan is a mixture of lime paste, betel nut and sometimes tobacco, wrapped up in a green betel leaf. People chew *pan* after a meal to help them digest their food. Varanasi is famous for its particular variety of *pan*. It is sold all over the city.

◄ *Snacks made of flour and chick peas. They are served with sour yoghurt, and puffy balls of bread called* poori.

▼ *The triangular betel leaves used for wrapping* pan. *The leaves are chewy but edible.*

Pan *is sold all over Varanasi. Here you can see it*
▼ *being prepared.*

Indian recipes

An Indian meal usually starts with a lot of tasty dishes in separate bowls, and ends with fresh fruit. Try making this simple Indian side-dish and drink for yourself. They are especially delicious on a hot summer's day.

Roadside stalls sell all sorts of delicious snacks. This is a bowl of spicy potato. In Hindi, the word for potato is aloo. *The red, pointed vegetables are hot chilli peppers. Fresh coriander (a type of herb) is sprinkled over the top.*

CUCUMBER RAITA

Ingredients
1 small cucumber, thinly sliced into strips
1 carton of plain, unsweetened yoghurt
1 tablespoon of lemon juice
1 teaspoonful of chopped mint
some black pepper
a tiny pinch of chilli powder

What to do
Put the yoghurt in a bowl and whisk it for two minutes with a fork. Add the other ingredients and mix well.

SWEET LASSI

Ingredients
300 ml plain, unsweetened yoghurt
300 ml milk
600 ml water
6 crushed ice cubes
3 teaspoonfuls of sugar
$^1/_2$ teaspoonful of chopped mint
a few chopped almonds

What to do
1 Mix the yoghurt, milk, water and three ice cubes together. Ask an adult to do this for you in an electric blender, if possible.
2 Add the mint, sugar and almonds and mix well. Serve with the other ice cubes.

Language and literature

The power of Sanskrit

Today, the main language spoken in Varanasi and right across north India is Hindi. India has another 13 official languages, including English, and hundreds of local **dialects**. But the language of ancient India was called Sanskrit. It was brought to India by the Aryans (see page 13).

The Hindu scriptures were originally written down in Sanskrit, although this was often hundreds of years after they had been composed. At first, they were passed on by word of mouth. Sanskrit was considered to be the sacred language of the gods and to have great power. It is a very exact, precise language. People believed that unless a prayer, for example, was spoken or pronounced absolutely correctly, it would have no effect.

Sanskrit later became the language of learning and scholarship. Like Latin, it is still studied but rarely spoken except on special occasions. It is related to Latin and Greek. The Hindi language grew out of Sanskrit and became the language of the ordinary people rather than of the priests and scholars.

The sacred texts

Unlike the Christian Bible or the Muslim Koran, there is no single holy book in Hinduism. Hindus have many sacred texts, including the *Vedas*, the *Upanishads* and the great **epic poems** of the *Ramayana* and the *Mahabharata*.

The Vedas The *Vedas* are the oldest of the Hindu sacred texts. They were used by the Aryans as long ago as 1500 BC, although they were not written down until hundreds of years later. The *Vedas* consist of hymns, prayers, magic spells, **commentaries** on the hymns, instructions for meditation and rules for performing sacrifices to the gods. They are concerned with the worship of the gods of nature, such as Indra, the god of thunder, Agni, the god of fire and Mitra, the Sun god. The oldest of the four *Vedas* is the *Rig Veda*, a collection of 1,028 hymns.

The Upanishads The *Upanishads* date from about 800 BC. They concentrate on the inner

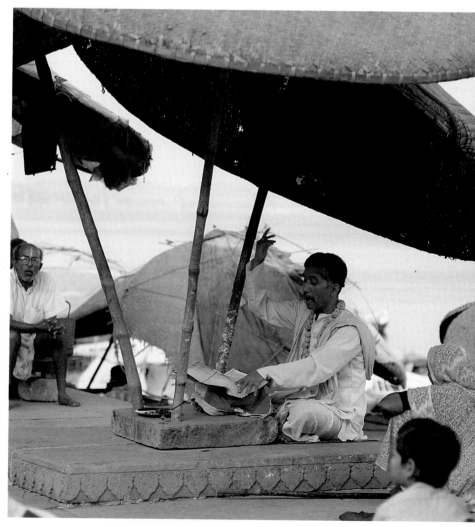

A Brahmin priest reciting passages from the Hindu holy books.

world of people's souls, rather than the outer world of nature that was dealt with in the *Vedas*. They stress the power of knowledge and meditation, rather than sacrifices. Some 112 *Upanishads* have been written down in Sanskrit. They use parables and stories to teach their message. The name *'Upanishad'* comes from the words *upa* which means 'near', *ni* which means 'down' and *shad* which means 'sit'. It refers to the way that pupils sat at their teachers' feet to listen to them.

Two epic poems

Two great epic poems are among the most important of the Hindu sacred texts. These are called the *Mahabharata* and the *Ramayana*. Hindu children hear the stories of these poems from the time they are very little.

The Mahabharata With some three million words, the *Mahabharata* is the longest poem ever composed. It tells the story of the war between two closely-related families, the Pandavas and the Kauravas. They fight for control of the kingdom of Hastinapura, which the Pandavas family finally wins.

The most important and most popular part of the *Mahabharata* is called the *Bhagavad Gita*, or 'Song of the Lord'. The setting for these verses is the battlefield, just before the battle begins. Arjuna, one the Pandavas, is in his chariot. He is riding with his charioteer, the god Krishna. He tells Krishna that it feels very wrong to be about to fight his own cousins. But Krishna replies that Arjuna must do his duty as a warrior, without thinking of how the end result might affect him. He persuades Arjuna that a person must not act selfishly. Instead, the way to salvation is through selfless action, devotion to duty and knowledge.

The Ramayana The *Ramayana* is celebrated every year in Varanasi, and all over India,

These texts are taken from the Upanishads *and can be found on the walls of the New Vishwanath Temple.*

with the performance of the Ram Lila plays (see page 31). The *Ramayana* tells the story of Rama, the human form taken by Vishnu on one of his visits to Earth. Rama is heir to the throne of the kingdom of Ayodhya, but he is robbed of this throne and sent into exile with his wife, Sita. Sita is kidnapped by Ravana, the demon king of Lanka. With the help of the monkey god, Hanuman, Rama rescues Sita and returns home to rule his kingdom wisely and fairly.

The *Ramayana* is thought to have been compiled by a wise man, called Valmiki, in about 300 BC. A Hindi version of the poem was written by the poet, Tulsi Das, in the 1570s while he was living in Varanasi. It is called the *Ram Charit Manas*, or the 'Lake of the Deeds of Rama'.

The monkey god, Hanuman, with Rama and Sita, close to his heart!

A passage from the Ram Charit Manas, *engraved on the marble walls of the Tulsi Manas Temple.*

Think and do

1 There are many different versions of the *Ramayana*. Try to tell the story in your own words. You could illustrate it with a picture of Hanuman and Rama rescuing Sita.

2 Why did Arjuna have to fight with his own feelings before he went into battle?

A centre of learning

Varanasi has been an important centre of learning and scholarship for many centuries. It has attracted teachers and pupils from all over India and the world. They come to study Sanskrit and the Hindu scriptures, and to continue the classical tradition of religious education for which Varanasi is famous.

Ashrams and monasteries

There are many *ashrams* at the tops of the *ghats* in Varanasi. An *ashram* is a mixture of a school, a university and a monastery. Traditionally, it is a place where religious teachers, called *gurus*, and their followers live. Brahmin children are also allowed to attend the *ashrams* for their education. The *ashrams* and monasteries in Varanasi are important shelters for wandering holy men, called *sannyasins*.

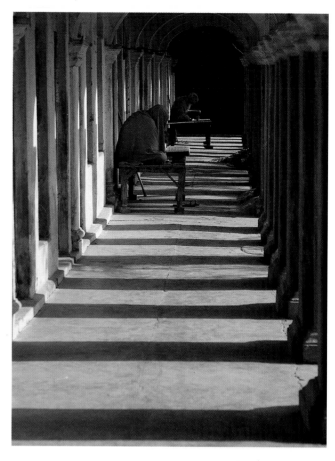

Sadhus *studying the holy books in an* ashram.

Brahmin children come from all over India to study in Varanasi's schools and ashrams.

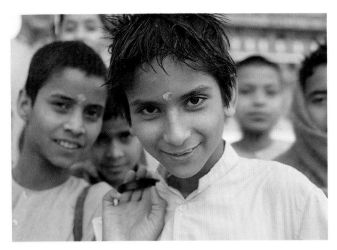
Young Brahmin students.

Sanskrit University

For hundreds of years, Varanasi has been the centre of Sanskrit study in north India. The Sanskrit University was founded by the British in the early 19th century. It is famous for its rare Sanskrit manuscripts and wise scholars and priests. The British encouraged the building of the University because they needed a ready team of scholars to help them understand Hindu laws. The Indian Government still goes to the University for advice.

The Benares Hindu University

The Benares Hindu University was founded by Pandit Madan Mohan Malaviya in 1916. He wanted to establish a modern university for the study of Hindu religion and culture, but there are also courses in medicine, engineering and business studies. The University stands on a huge semi-circle of land given by the Maharaja of Varanasi. It is one of the biggest universities in Asia.

Writers and philosophers

During the 15th and 16th centuries, several great poets lived in Varanasi. The poet, Kabir, was born into a poor Muslim family. But he believed very strongly that all religions were equal and his work was influenced not only by Islam, but by Hinduism and Buddhism as well. People still sing songs written by Kabir.

Tulsi Das (1543-1623) was a follower of Rama (see page 41). Very little is known of his life but it is thought that he was born in Ayodhya into a Brahmin family. However, his parents died when he was still quite young and he was forced to live by begging. He later decided to devote his whole life to Rama, so he moved to Varanasi, where he completed his famous Hindi version of Rama's life, the *Ram Charit Manas*. People believe that he was a great saint and wise man.

Founders and reformers

Two great teachers and **reformers** visited Varanasi in about 500 BC – the Buddha, who founded Buddhism, and Mahavira, the founder of the Jain religion.

The Buddha preached his first sermon in the Deer Park at Sarnath, about 10 kilometres away from Varanasi. A huge shrine, called the Dhamekh Stupa, is thought to stand on

Pandit Madan Mohan Malaviya, the founder of the Benares Hindu University.

the spot where he taught. The Buddha urged people to follow a 'Middle Path' of **moderation** and **compromise** which would lead to *nirvana*, or salvation. Sarnath became, and remains, a sacred site for Buddhists. Although its buildings now lie in ruins, it is a quiet, peaceful place to visit.

The Jain religion was founded at about the same time as Buddhism by a man called Mahavira. He was the last of the Jain teachers, known as *Tirthankars*, or 'finders of the path'. Jains believe strongly in the value of all living things. They are strict vegetarians, and some devout Jains even cover their mouths so that they do not swallow insects accidentally. Their temples are extremely well looked after.

Over the centuries, many religions have been allowed to flourish in Varanasi. Nowadays, it is the Hindu religion which fills the city with its special atmosphere.

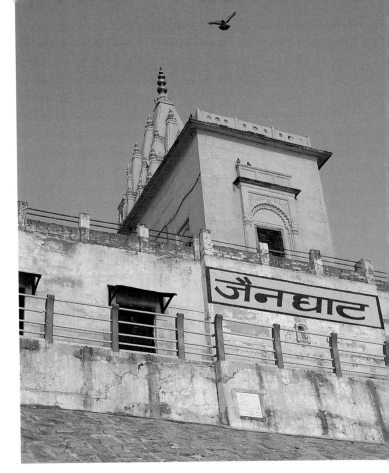

A Jain temple on Jain Ghat.

Buddhist pilgrims praying in the Mulgandha Kuti-Wihar temple in Sarnath.

Images of the Tirthankars *inside a Jain temple.*

Key words

reformers   people who change ideas and ways of behaving

moderation   behaviour or opinions that are not too extreme

compromise   a solution to a problem that satisfies everyone

Important events in Hinduism

The following are some important events with the dates on which they occurred:

BC BEFORE THE BIRTH OF CHRIST
2500 The Indus Valley civilization is at the height of its power
1500 The Aryans begin to arrive in India
1500–1000 The *Rig Veda* is compiled; the caste system develops
800–400 The *Upanishads* are composed
500 The Buddha teaches at Sarnath and all over India; Jainism is founded by Mahavira
486 Death of the Buddha
268–231 Reign of King Ashoka

AD AFTER THE BIRTH OF CHRIST
300BC– The *Mahabharata* and the
AD 300 *Ramayana* are composed
100 Indian religious ideas begin to spread to South East Asia
320–475 The Gupta dynasty rules; Hindu culture and religion flourishes
800 Shankaracharya, the Hindu philosopher, teaches

1050 The Hindu philosopher, Ramanuja, teaches
From The Muslims begin to invade
1000 India and spread the Islamic religion
1469 Birth of Guru Nanak, founder of the Sikh religion
1500s Devotional worship of Rama and Krishna flourishes
1570s Tulsi Das writes the *Ram Charit Manas*
1700s– The British and other European
1800s powers bring Christianity to India
1850– The rise of Hindu religious
1900s reform movements, such as the Arya Samaj, Brahmo Samaj and the Ramakrishna Mission
1915 Mahatma Gandhi returns to India from South Africa to lead India's struggle for independence from British rule; he campaigns for religious tolerance
1947 India gains independence but is divided into largely Hindu India and mostly Muslim Pakistan

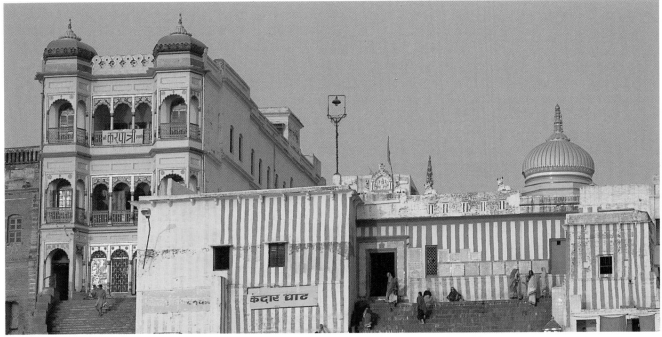

The Shiva temple and ashram *on Kedar Ghat.*

Further Reading

For younger readers
The Hindu World Patricia Bahree (Simon and Schuster)

Focus on India Shahrukh Husain (Evans Brothers Limited)

Country Fact Files: India Anita Ganeri/Jonardon Ganeri (Simon and Schuster)

Living Festivals series Sauresh Ray (Pergamon Press Limited)

Religions through Festivals: Hinduism Robert Jackson (Longman)

Seasons of Splendour Madhur Jaffrey (Puffin Books)

For older readers
A History of India Romila Thapar (Pelican Books)

The Upanishads (Penguin Classics)

The Bhagavad Gita (Penguin Classics)

Benares Henry Wilson (Thames and Hudson)

Hinduism K.M. Sen (Pelican Books)

Index